By the same author
Merde Encore!
(also published by Angus & Robertson)

MERDE!

GENEVIÈVE

Illustrated by
MICHAEL HEATH

The REAL French You Were Never Taught at School

A division of HarperCollins *Publishers*

AN ANGUS & ROBERTSON BOOK

Angus & Robertson (UK)
16 Golden Square, London, W1R 4BN
United Kingdom
Collins/Angus & Robertson Publishers Australia
A division of HarperCollins Publishers
(Australia) Pty Ltd
Unit 4, Eden Park, 31 Waterloo Road,
North Ryde, NSW 2113, Australia
William Collins Publishers Ltd 31 View Road,
Glenfield, Auckland 10, New Zealand

First published in Australia by
Angus & Robertson Australia in 1984
First published in the United Kingdom by
Angus & Robertson (UK) in 1984
Reprinted 1984, 1985 (twice), 1986,
1987, 1988 (twice), 1989, 1990

Copyright © Geneviève Edis 1984

National Library of Australia
Cataloguing-in-publication data.

Geneviève, 1947–
  Merde!
  ISBN 0 207 14910 0.
  1. French language–Slang–Dictionaries.
  2. French language–Dictionaries–English
  I. Heath, Michael.   II. Title.
447.09

Typeset in 10pt Palatino by
Graphicraft Typesetters Ltd
Printed in England by Clays Ltd, St Ives plc

A mes vieux (René et Nanette)
A mon frangin (Hervé)
A mon mec (Richard)
A mes gosses (Rupert, Oliver et Jamyn)

CONTENTS

PREFACE

Do you remember when you were learning French at school and looked in vain through your dictionary for all the dirty words? Have you thought you had a reasonable command of the language, then seen a French film or gone to France, only to find that you could barely understand a word? You were, of course, never taught *real* French by your boring teachers who failed to give you the necessary tools of communication while stuffing the subjunctive imperfect down your throat. French "argot" (slang) is not just the dirty words (though, have no fear, you will find them here), it is an immensely rich language with its own words for very ordinary things, words that are in constant use. Here, then, is not an exhaustive or scholarly dictionary of "argot" (that would be ten times thicker) but a guide to survival in understanding everyday French as it is *really* spoken.

Guidance

Asterisks after "argot" words indicate a degree of rudeness above the ordinary colloquial. Two asterisks show a whopper, although you should not assume that strength and rudeness cause a word to be used less frequently, "au contraire" . . .

When an English definition is underlined, that definition gives a good equivalent flavour, feeling and degree of rudeness of the French word. Good equivalents are not that common, so rely generally on the English definition for the meaning of the French word, on the asterisks for its strength and on the many examples for its usage. Just remember, to be authentic is to be rude.

I THE MUSTS

Common Everyday Musts

So many everyday words have their colloquial counterparts which appear constantly in conversation. The following is a list of the most frequently used and, therefore, most necessary ones, which do not fall into any of the neat categories of subsequent sections.

NECESSARY NOUNS

People

a fellow, a guy, a man	un type
	un gars
	un mec*
a woman	une bonne femme*
a bird, a chick, a broad	une gonzesse**
a kid	un/une môme
	un/une gosse
	un gamin, une gamine
what's-his-name	machin, machin-chouette
what's-her-name	machine, machine-chouette
a friend	un copain, une copine
Mrs, Miss, ma	la mère (la mère Dupont a dit = ma Dupont said)
Mr, pa, old man	le père (le père Dupont = old man Dupont)
parents	les vieux

1

the old man (father)	le paternel
	le vieux
the old lady (mother)	la maternelle
	la vieille
a son	un fiston
son! young man! junior! (USA)	fiston!
a brother	un frangin
a sister	une frangine
a beastly person	un chameau (literally, a camel)

a bastard	un salaud** (ce salaud de Dupont = that bastard Dupont) un salopard**
a bitch	une salope** (cette salope de Marie = that bitch Marie)
a bastard or a bitch	une vache* (literally, a cow) une peau de vache* (literally, a cow's hide)
a shit	un fumier* (literally, manure)
an arse-licker	un lèche-cul**
a boot-licker	un lèche-bottes*

Animals

a dog, a mutt (USA)	un cabot* un klebs* un klébard*
a bird	un piaf* (remember Edith Piaf?)

Things

nothing	quedale, or que dalle
a book	un bouquin
a car	une bagnole
an old banger	un tacot
a slow vehicle	un veau (literally, a calf)
a fag (the one you smoke)	une sèche
water	la flotte
paper	du papelard
a rag (newspaper)	une feuille de chou (literally, a cabbage leaf) un canard

3

a <u>bike</u>	une bécane
	un vélo
a <u>pad</u> (room)	une piaule
the <u>sack</u> (bed)	le pieu
	le plumard (from "la plume" = the feather)
a lamp	une loupiote
the <u>telly</u>, the <u>box</u>	la télé
a phone call	un coup de fil
a boat	un rafiot
a thing, a <u>thingummyjig</u>	un bidule
	un truc
	un machin
	un fourbi
	un engin
the <u>loo</u>, the <u>can</u> (USA)	les water (from "les WC" = the water-closet)
	les chiottes**
a snag	un pépin
a mess, a shambles	la pagaille, la pagaïe
a <u>balls-up</u>, a mess	un bordel**

Clothes

clothes	les frusques (m.)
	les fringues (f.)
	les nippes (f.)
a hat	un bitos
	un galurin
a suit	un costard
a pair of trousers	un falzar
a shirt	une liquette

4

a raincoat	un imper (short for "un imperméable")
shoes	les godasses (f.) les pompes (f.) les tatanes (f.)
outsize shoes	les écrase-merde** (f.) (literally, shit-squashers)
an umbrella	un pépin un pébroque
a ring	une bagouse
a suitcase	une valoche

NECESSARY ADJECTIVES

friendly and nice	sympa (short for "sympathique")
exhausting	crevant,e
killingly funny	crevant,e tordant,e
funny	rigolo, rigolote
disgusting	dégueulasse* débectant,e* (from "débecter*" = to <u>puke</u>)
ugly; lousy	moche
useless, no good	à la gomme à la noix

NECESSARY VERBS

to understand	piger
to not understand a damn thing about	ne piger quedale à

5

to <u>dig up</u>, to find	dégoter, dégotter
to lose	paumer
to watch out for, to be careful about	faire gaffe à
to make a mistake	faire une gaffe (note the difference from the preceding expression) se gourer
to <u>bust</u>	bousiller péter*
to have some nerve, to be cheeky	avoir du culot être culotté,e avoir du toupet être gonflé,e (literally, to be swollen)
to go too far, to push things	charrier

6

to be an enthusiast, to be crazy (about)	être un fana, une fana ("fana" is short for "fanatique"; c'est un fana de la voile = he's crazy about sailing)
to have a good time, to laugh	rigoler se marrer
to kid, to joke	rigoler (tu rigoles, non? = are you kidding?)
to grouse	rouspéter (gives "un rouspéteur, une rouspéteuse" = a moaner, grumbler) râler (gives "un râleur, une râleuse" = a moaner, grumbler)
to be in a good mood	être de bon poil être bien vissé,e (literally, to be well screwed in) être bien luné,e
to be in a bad mood	être de mauvais poil être mal vissé,e être mal luné,e
to not make much of an effort	ne pas se fouler
to be lucky	avoir du bol avoir du pot
to be unlucky	manquer de bol manquer de pot
to nick, to pinch (to steal)	chiper pincer piquer faucher barboter rafler
to lick someone's boots	faire de la lèche à quelqu'un*
to be pouring with rain	flotter

7

to be landed with	se farcir*

NECESSARY BITS AND PIECES

yes	ouais
OK	d'ac (short for "d'accord")
no way!	des clous! tintin!
so what?	et alors? ben quoi? (ben = eh bien)
damn!	zut! la barbe!
goddammit! oh my God!	putain**! (literally, whore)
that damn ..., that bloody ...	ce putain de ..., cette putaine de ...**
you ...	espèce de ... (espèce de salaud = you bastard)
you ... (pl.)	bande de ... (bande d'idiots = you bunch of idiots)
extremely + an adjective	archi- (archi-dégueulasse = extremely disgusting)
very, really	vachement drôlement rudement
shut up!	écrase*! ferme-la*! ta gueule**! ("gueule" is literally an animal's mouth, but is used pejoratively for people's mouths or faces)
I dare you!	chiche!

<u>my arse</u>!	mon cul**!
hi!	salut!
this afternoon	c't'aprèm (short for "cet après-midi)
what? <u>huh</u>?	hein?
<u>phew</u>!	ouf!
ow, <u>ouch</u>!	aie! ouille!
<u>yuk</u>!	beurk!

A FEW TIPS FOR CONSTRUCTING AUTHENTIC-SOUNDING SENTENCES

- Clip the end vowel off pronouns. Say "t'es sympa" instead of "tu es sympa".
- "Ce," "cet," and "cette" are clipped to become "c'", "c't" and "c'te". Say "c'mec" (pronounced "smec") instead of "ce mec".
- Use "y'a" for "il y a" and "y'avait" for "il y avait".
- Omit the "ne" from the negative "ne ... pas". Say "j'sais pas" (pronounced "chais pas") instead of "je ne sais pas".
- Emphasise the subject by adding the relevant indirect pronoun at the end of the sentence. Say "j'sais pas, moi", "t'as du pot, toi". Or stress the subject by adding the noun that a subject pronoun connotes. Say "elles sont moches, ces godasses", "il est gonflé, c'mec".

NOW TRY YOUR HAND AT THE FOLLOWING SENTENCES

1 C't'espèce de salaud de frangin de Jojo m'a piqué ma bécane. Il a du toupet, c'mec.

2 "Passe-moi un coup de fil c't'aprèm." "D'ac."

3 Oh, putain, j'ai bousillé la bagnole du paternel.

4 Ton copain est vachement sympa, hein?

5   Aie! Fais gaffe, tu m'fais mal!

6   Il est pas rigolo, le gars. Il est toujours de mauvais poil.

7   J'pige quedale à c'bouquin, moi.

8   Allez, venez, les gars, à la flotte!

9   C'est moche; la mère machine-chouette a paumé son cabot.

10 Où est-ce que t'as dégotté c'truc dégueulasse?

11 Tu charries, ta piaule est un vrai bordel.

1   That Jojo's bastard of a brother has nicked my bike. That guy has got some nerve.

2   "Give me a ring this afternoon." "OK."

3   Oh, hell, I've busted my old man's car.

4   Your friend is really nice, isn't he?

5   Ouch! Watch it, you're hurting me!

6   That fellow isn't much fun. He's always in a bad mood.

7   I don't get a damn thing about this book.

8   Hey, come on fellows, let's jump in (that is, in the water)!

9   It's too bad; old ma what's-her-name has lost her dog.

10 Where did you find that disgusting thing?

11 It's a bit much, your room is a real mess.

The Absolute Musts

The MERDE** Family

"Merde**" means literally and figuratively "shit". It is known in polite circles as "les cinq lettres" (as we would say "a four-letter word"). But then, there are few such circles, and the word is vital for communication with the natives. It does not have the impact and shock value of its English equivalent, so sprinkle liberally. The "merde**" family has several nominal, adjectival and verbal forms, so it can be, and is, handily inserted anywhere and anyhow.

NOUNS

la merde** = the <u>shit</u>
as in:

J'ai marché dans de la merde**.
I walked in some <u>dogshit</u>.

Oh, merde** alors!
Oh, shit! Oh, hell! Oh, damn!

and in the expressions:

être dans la merde**
<u>to be up shit creek</u>

se foutre** **dans la merde****
to get it all wrong (literally, to put oneself in the shit)

ne pas se prendre pour de la petite merde**
to take oneself very seriously, to think oneself great (literally, to not take oneself for small shit)

11

un emmerdement** = a real problem, trouble

J'ai des emmerdements** avec ma bagnole.
I'm having real trouble with my car.

un emmerdeur, une emmerdeuse** = a pain in the neck

Ce type est un emmerdeur** de premier ordre.
That fellow is a first-class pain in the neck.

le merdier** = a fine mess, a jam, a fix (literally, the shitpile)

T'es dans un de ces merdiers**, toi alors!
You sure are in a fine mess!

un petit merdeux, une petite merdeuse** = a little twerp

Le môme du père Dupont est un vrai petit merdeux**.
Old man Dupont's kid is a real little twerp.

un démerdeur, une démerdeuse** = one who always manages,
one who always gets what he/she wants (literally, one who always
gets out of the shit)

J'ai jamais vu une démerdeuse** comme Pascale.
I've never known anyone always to get her own way like
Pascale.

la démerde** = the art of being resourceful, of always landing on
one's feet, of always getting what one wants (the French do
consider this, known also as "le système D", an art form)

Ce mec* est un champion de la démerde**.
This fellow is a master at landing on his feet.

merde! = good luck! (before a challenge, such as an exam)

Bon, allez, merde, ça ira!
Well, good luck, it'll be OK!

ADJECTIVES

emmerdant,e** = annoying, irritating, boring, a <u>pain in the neck</u>

Qu'est-ce qu'il est emmerdant** ton frangin!
What a pain your brother is!

emmerdé,e** = worried, annoyed

12

J'suis drôlement emmerdé**, j'ai paumé mon imper.
I'm really annoyed, I've lost my raincoat.

VERBS

emmerder** = to annoy, to irritate, to <u>give someone a pain in the neck</u>

Elle m'emmerde** cette bonne femme*, elle n'arrête pas de râler.
That woman gets on my nerves, she never stops complaining.

and in the expression:

Je l'emmerde**, **je les emmerde****.
To hell with him/her, to hell with them.

s'emmerder** = to be bored stiff

Qu'est-ce qu'on s'emmerde** ici.
What a bore it is here.

se démerder** = to manage, to get by

Ma copine se démerde** toujours pour avoir les meilleures places.
My girlfriend always manages to get the best seats.

13

The CHIER** Family

Anal matters again! Draw your own conclusions about their importance in the French language and psyche. "Chier**" means literally "to crap". The family of words derives from this meaning but has expanded to express intense annoyance and irritation. "Chiant**", for example, is one step further in rudeness than "emmerdant**", as "pain in the arse" is stronger than "pain in the neck".

VERBS

chier** = to <u>crap</u>

Son sale cabot a chié** partout dans ma piaule.
Her rotten old dog crapped all over my room.

faire chier** = to <u>give a real pain in the arse</u>

Ma maternelle me fait chier**.
My mother gives me a real pain in the arse.

envoyer chier quelqu'un** = to tell someone to fuck off

Un de ces jours, je vais envoyer mon vieux chier**.
One of these days I'm going to tell my old man to fuck off.

NOUNS

la chiasse** = the runs, and thence, fear

Rien que de penser aux examens, il a la chiasse**.
Just thinking about exams gives him the runs.

les chiottes** (f.) = the bog (UK), the can (USA)

C'est par là, les chiottes**?
Is the bog that way?

une chierie** = a whole mess of problems; a drag

Quelle chierie**, l'école!
What a drag school is!

ADJECTIVE

chiant,e** = extremely irritating, boring, a <u>pain in the arse</u>

14

Elle est chiante**, cette môme.
That kid is a real pain in the arse.

C'est chiant**, ça.
That's a real drag.

The CON** Family

Physically, we haven't moved too far away, as we reach the third absolutely vital must. "Con**" means literally "cunt", but is used constantly and emphatically to indicate stupidity, thickness, somewhat as Americans use "asshole". As with "merde" and "chier", "con**" is everywhere in conversation and gives rise to a family of words.

NOUNS

un con, un connard**
une conne, une connasse, une connarde** = an idiot, a jerk, a fool

Quel con**, ce mec*!
What a damn fool that fellow is!

une connerie** = a stupidity; rubbish

Ma frangine ne fait que des conneries**.
My sister does nothing but stupid things.

C'est de la vraie connerie**, ce bouquin.
This book is a load of rubbish.

ADJECTIVES

con, conne**
connard, connarde** = stupid, thick, dumb

Les filles sont connes**.
Girls are real idiots.

Il a l'air con**.
He looks stupid.

VERBS

déconner** = to fool about; to do foolish things; to talk rubbish

Hé, les gosses, vous avez fini de déconner**?
Hey, kids, have you finished fooling about?

Ce machin déconne**.
This thing is going bonkers.

faire le con** = to act stupidly

Faut toujours qu'il fasse le con**, ce mec*.
That fellow can never act sensibly.

The FICHER* and FOUTRE** Families

The verbs "ficher*" and "foutre**" are very useful and necessary: they can mean "to do", "to give", "to put", and they figure in many vivid expressions. "Foutre**" is the stronger of the two. Learn their usage through these examples; for the sake of easy reading, only "foutre**" will be used but, remember, either verb works.

VERBS

foutre** = to do
ne rien foutre** = to not do a damn thing

Qu'est-ce que tu fous**?
What the hell are you doing?

Mon frangin ne fout** rien en classe.
My brother doesn't do a damn thing in class.

foutre** **une baffe** = to give a slap

Arrête ou je te fous** une baffe.
Quit it or I'll slap you.

foutre** **la paix à quelqu'un** = to leave someone alone

Foutez-nous** la paix!
Leave us alone!

foutre** **la trouille à quelqu'un** = to scare the hell out of someone

Ce klebs* a l'air enragé: il me fout** la trouille.
This dog looks rabid: it scares the hell out of me.

foutre** = to put

16

Où as-tu foutu** les clefs de la maison?
Where the hell did you put the house keys?

foutre le camp** = to push off, to get the hell out

Allez, foutez-moi** le camp d'ici, bande de voyous.
Go on, push off, you hooligans.

Hé, les gars, foutons** le camp avant que les flics n'arrivent.
Hey, you guys, let's push off before the fuzz comes.

foutre au panier** = to bung in the waste paper basket, to chuck
out

Un de ces jours, j'vais foutre** la télé au panier.
One of these days I'm going to chuck the telly out.

foutre en l'air** = to chuck out, to ruin

La maternelle a foutu** toutes mes vieilles godasses en l'air.
My mother chucked all my old shoes out.

Le mauvais temps a foutu** tous nos plans en l'air.
The bad weather ruined all our plans.

foutre à la porte** = to kick out; to sack

Ses vieux l'ont foutu** à la porte.
His parents kicked him out of the house.

Son patron l'a foutu** à la porte.
His boss sacked him.

se foutre de quelqu'un** = to take the mickey out of someone, to
make fun of someone; to take someone for a ride, to rip someone
off

Mes copains se sont foutus** de mon falzar.
My friends made fun of my trousers.

Il s'est foutu** de toi le mec* qui t'a vendu cette bagnole.
The fellow who sold you this car took you for a ride.

se foutre de la gueule** des gens, se foutre** de la poire* du
monde** = to take everyone for a damn idiot

Quoi, quinze francs pour un café? Vous vous foutez** de la
gueule** des gens, non?
What, fifteen francs for a cup of coffee? You've got to be
kidding!

s'en foutre** de = to not give a damn about

Je m'en fous** de ce que tu en penses.
I don't give a damn what you think about it.

se foutre** dedans = to make a real mess (of something), to make a mistake

Cette fois-ci, il s'est vraiment foutu** dedans.
This time he really put his foot in it.
(The French and the English expressions both imply stepping into something nasty.)

se foutre** parterre = to fall flat on one's face

Fais gaffe, tu vas te foutre** parterre!
Watch it, you're going to fall flat on your face!

The following two expressions are used only as given here:

Ça la fout** mal = It's a damned awkward situation.

Va te/Allez vous faire foutre**! = <u>Piss off! Fuck off! Get stuffed!</u>

The participles "**fichu,e***" and "**foutu,e****" can also mean "done for", "finished", "ruined".

La télé est foutue**.
The telly has had it.

ADJECTIVES

The adjectival forms, "fichu,e*" and "foutu,e**", are used in the following expressions:

être mal foutu,e** = to feel rotten, ill; to work badly, to be badly set up

J'vais pas en classe aujourd'hui, j'suis mal foutu**.
I'm not going to school today, I feel lousy.

Ce magasin est mal foutu**.
This shop is badly laid out.

être bien foutu,e** = to have a great body; to work well, to be well set up

Elle est vachement bien foutue**, ta frangine.
Your sister sure has a great body.

Cette bagnole est drôlement bien foutue**.
This car is really nifty.

être foutu,e** de faire quelque chose = to be liable to do something

Fais gaffe, il est foutu** de tout bousiller.
Watch it, he's liable to bust everything.

ne même pas être foutu,e** de faire quelque chose = to not even be capable of doing something, to not even be willing to do something

Il n'est même pas foutu** de lui envoyer une carte pour son anniversaire.
He can't even be bothered to send her a card for her birthday.

"**Fichu,e***" and "**foutu,e****" are used as "damned", "bloody", etc.

Ce foutu** temps est déprimant.
This bloody weather is depressing.

19

NOUNS

Two nouns belong to the foutre** family only:

le foutoir** = a shambles, a mess

Ta piaule est un vrai foutoir**
Your room is a real mess.

la foutaise** = a load of old rubbish

C'est de la foutaise**, ton truc.
That thing of yours is a load of old rubbish.

II VARIATIONS ON A THEME

Fact: the French individual feels superior to his fellow man, foreign or not. Consequence: the French have a very wide selection of words to express their contempt for the intellectual, mental or spiritual inferiority of others as well as their annoyance derived from this contempt. The two following sections give you the range of words to which you might be subjected. The third offers a few replies.

Theme One: What an Idiot

a jerk, an idiot, a fool

un con, une conne**, un connard, une connarde**, une connasse** (remember chapter I?)
un couillon** (from "les couilles**" (f.) = testicles)

crazy, <u>cracked</u>, <u>bonkers</u>, <u>nuts</u>

dingue
dingo
cinglé,e
zinzin
timbré,e
sonné,e
siphonné,e
tapé,e
piqué,e
toqué,e
maboul,e
loufoque
marteau
malade

21

All these and the following adjectives except "marteau" can be used as nouns when preceded by an article. For example,

C'est un vrai cinglé, ce type.
That fellow is a real nutcase.

Où as-tu dégotté une dingue pareille?
Where did you pick up such a crazy woman?

half-witted, mentally defective	débile demeuré,e arriéré,e crétin,e
a half-wit, a mental defective	un débile mental, une débile mentale un minus
degenerate	dégénéré,e taré,e
dim	paumé,e (remember "paumer" = to lose)
a clot, a twit	une andouille un corniaud une cruche une gourde un pied une patate
a nitwit	un ballot
silly	bébête cucul* (cucul la praline* = silly billy)
a silly goose	une bécasse
thick, dumb	con, conne** bouché,e
gaga , senile	gaga gâteux, gâteuse
weird	tordu,e

a scatterbrain	une tête de linotte
to go off one's rocker, to go round the twist	dérailler (literally, to go off the rails) débloquer ne pas tourner rond
to have a screw loose	avoir une case de vide, (literally, to have an empty compartment) être tombé,e sur le crâne (literally, to have fallen on one's skull)
to be as thick as two posts	être con comme un balai** être con comme la lune* (this particular "lune" being not the moon, but the backside)
are you crazy?	ça va pas, non?

To lessen the offensiveness of a term, you can use "un peu ... sur les bords". For example,

Elle est un peu zinzin sur les bords.
She's a bit on the cracked side (literally, she's a bit cracked around the edges).

Theme Two: What a Pain

He/she is a real pain	Il/elle est casse-pieds Il/elle est emmerdant,e** Il/elle est chiant,e**
irritating	enquiquinant,e empoisonnant,e
boring	barbant,e rasant,e rasoir
to bore	barber raser (literally, to shave, and the

shaving imagery to indicate boredom gives rise to an important gesture that you should be able to interpret. If you see a Frenchman raise his arm and stroke his cheek with the back of his fingers, you will know that he is indicating his boredom and irritation with a person or a situation.)

deadly boring	assommant,e (assommer = to knock out)
to get on someone's nerves	taper quelqu'un sur les nerfs casser les pieds de quelqu'un les casser à quelqu'un (the "les" can refer to "pieds" or "couilles**")
to <u>give someone a pain in the neck, arse; to piss someone off</u>	faire suer quelqu'un (suer = perspire) faire chier quelqu'un** emmerder quelqu'un**
to irritate	enquiquiner empoisonner
to be fed up with	en avoir marre de en avoir plein le dos de en avoir ras le bol de en avoir plein le cul de**
<u>What a drag</u>!	quelle barbe!
to not be able to stand someone	ne pas pouvoir sentir quelqu'un ne pas pouvoir piffer quelqu'un* ne pas pouvoir blairer quelqu'un* ("le pif*" and "le blair*" mean the <u>conk</u>. These three expressions therefore literally mean "not to be able to smell someone," reminding us of the prominence of French noses.)

24

to not be able to stand someone	ne pas pouvoir voir quelqu'un ne pas pouvoir voir quelqu'un en peinture ne pas pouvoir encaisser quelqu'un
to disgust	débecter*

Theme Three: I Don't Give a Damn

I don't give a damn	je m'en fiche* je m'en fous** je m'en contrefiche* je m'en contrefous** je m'en balance* je m'en bats l'oeil*
I don't give a fuck	je m'en branle** (branler** = to masturbate; this expression is rather strong!)

To say that you don't give a damn about a certain thing, use any of the above followed by "de" and the object of your indifference. For example,

Je m'en fous de ton programme de télé, finis tes devoirs d'abord.
I don't give a damn about your TV programme, finish your homework first.

REVISION

Just a few sentences to see if you have absorbed the previous vocabulary.

1 Une gonzesse plutôt conne sortait avec un mec vachement sympa. Mais le type commençait à en avoir marre d'elle parce qu'elle pigeait jamais rien. Un jour, il en avait vraiment ras le bol. Il lui a dit de foutre le camp. "T'as du toupet," dit-elle, en lui foutant une baffe. La garce a appelé son cabot, en plus, pour déchirer le falzar du gars, ce qui l'a vraiment fait chier. "Salope!" cria-t-il, "Va te faire foutre!"

25

2   Je peux pas blairer ce débile de Jojo. Il emmerde le monde avec tous ses problèmes.

3   Les anglais sont complètement dingues, ils conduisent leurs bagnoles du mauvais côté.

4   C'est toujours les plus cons qui se prennent pas pour de la petite merde.

1   A pretty thick woman was going out with some really nice guy. But the fellow was beginning to get fed up with her because she never understood anything. One day, he'd really had it. He told her to push off. "You've got a cheek," she said, slapping him. What's more, the cow called her dog to tear the guy's trousers, which really pissed him off. "You bitch!" he yelled, "Fuck off!"

2   I can't stand that half-wit Jojo. He bugs everyone with all his problems.

3   The English are really crazy, they drive their cars on the wrong side.

4   It's always the dumbest who think they're so great.

Now, if you have mastered the previous chapters, we can begin to have fun, what with the body and sex coming up.

III THE BODY AND ITS FUNCTIONS

The Parts

the body	la carcasse (mainly in the expression "bouge ta carcasse" = budge, move!)
the head	le caillou (particularly in the expression "pas un poil sur le caillou" = as bald as a coot, literally, not a hair on the stone) le crâne (literally, the skull)
the <u>nut</u>	la citrouille (literally, the pumpkin)
the brain, the head	le ciboulot
the brain	les méninges (mainly in the expression "se creuser les méninges" = to rack one's brain)
the <u>mug</u> , the face	la gueule** la tronche* la bouille la trogne*
hair	les tifs (m.)
the <u>conk</u>, the nose	le pif* le blair*
the eyes	les mirettes (f.)
the ears	les esgourdes (f.)

27

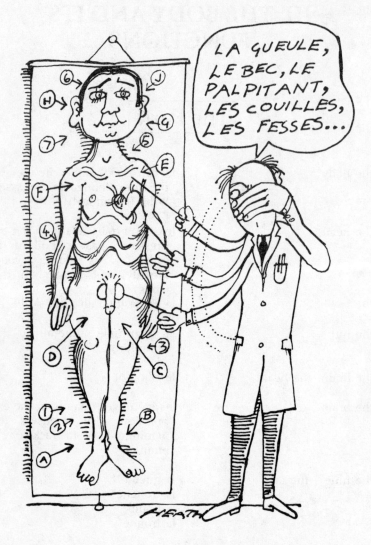

the mouth	le bec* (literally, the beak)
	la gueule**
the lips	les babines (f.)
the moustache	les bacchantes (f.)
the beard	la barbouze

the hand	la paluche*
	la pince (serrer la pince = to shake hands)
	la patte* (bas les pattes* = hands off)
the biceps (muscles)	les biscoteaux (m.)
the leg	la patte*
	la guibole*
the <u>pins</u>	les quilles* (f.)
the thighs (heavy female ones)	les jambons* (m.; literally, the hams)
	les gigots* (m.; literally, the legs of lamb)
the foot	le panard*
the <u>ticker</u> (heart)	le palpitant
the <u>guts</u>	les boyaux* (m.)
	les tripes* (f.)
the <u>belly</u>	le bide*
	le bidon*
the paunch	la bedaine
	la brioche

AND NOW THOSE WORDS YOU'VE BEEN LOOKING ALL OVER FOR

the <u>tits</u>	les nichons* (m.)
	les miches* (f.)
	les tétons* (m.)
	les doudounes* (f.)
the genital organ, male or female	le zizi (a word used from early childhood onwards)
the <u>dick</u>	la kiquette*, la quéquette*

29

the <u>cock</u>	la bitte** la queue** (literally, the tail) la verge** (literally, the rod) le zob** la pine**
the <u>balls</u>	les couilles** (f.)
the <u>family jewels</u>	les bijoux de famille
the <u>pussy</u>	le chat* la chatte* le con**
the clit	la praline* ("praline" is a sugared almond and the use of the word for clit comes from the similarity in shape)
the bottom, the <u>bum</u>, the <u>backside</u>	l'arrière-train les fesses* (f.; a useful expression to describe others, not yourself, is "avoir le feu aux fesses*" = to be in a hurry) le derche
the <u>arse</u>	la lune* le cul** ("le papier-cul**" or "pécu**" from the initial "p" for "papier" + "cul**" = toilet paper, <u>bogroll</u>)
the <u>rump</u>	la croupe*
the <u>arsehole</u>	le trou de balle**

Bodily Functions

to cry	chialer*
to be tired	être crevé,e être vanné,e

30

LE BEAU CHAT

to be <u>washed out</u>	être lessivé,e (la lessive = the washing)
to sleep	roupiller pioncer
to take a catnap	pousser un roupillon
to <u>be dying of cold, heat, hunger, thirst</u>	crever de froid, de chaud, de faim, de soif

to be cold	cailler (as in "je caille" = I'm freezing)
to catch a cold	attraper la crève
to be ill	avoir la crève
to puke	dégobiller* dégueuler**
to grow old, to be getting on	prendre de la bouteille prendre du bouchon
to kick the bucket, to snuff it, to die	crever* (note the versatility of the word which literally means "to burst" and make sure you learn the variations of use above as they do make for variations of meaning) caner* claquer* clamecer* casser sa pipe
a stiff (corpse)	un macchabée, un macab*
to stink (applied only to living creatures)	puer le bouc (literally, to smell of goat) puer le fauve (literally, to smell of wild animal)
to stink (generally applicable)	puer cocoter* fouetter* schlinguer*
to burp	roter
to piss	pisser* faire pipi (the childish term)
to crap	chier** faire caca (the childish term)
to wipe one's arse	se torcher le cul**

shit	la merde**
turds	les étrons (m.)
to fart	péter* (this verb gives rise to a few useful expressions:

péter plus haut que son cul** = to think too highly of oneself; literally, to fart higher than one's arse

péter le feu* = to be full of energy; literally, to fart fire

un pète-sec* = a strict disciplinarian; literally, a clean, dry farter

a fart	un pet*
to have a hard-on	bander** avoir la tringle**
to jerk oneself off, to masturbate	se branler** se tripoter*

Body Types

to be striking	avoir de la gueule
a handsome young thing (male)	un beau gosse
to be well endowed (both sexes)	être bien monté,e
naked	à poil
a beanpole (both sexes)	une grande asperge une grande bringue une grande perche
a puny runt	un avorton** (literally, the left-over from an abortion) un résidu de fausse couche** (literally, the leftover from a miscarriage)
a midget	un nabot
a skinny bones	un maigrichon, une maigri-chonne
as thin as a rake	maigre comme un clou
a hulking great brute	une armoire à glace (literally, a wardrobe) un balaise un malabar
big, large	mastoc maousse

brawny, well-built	baraqué,e
a big, tough guy	un casseur (literally, one who breaks things)
a big woman, a <u>horse</u>	un grand cheval une jument (literally, a mare)
a dumpy little woman	un pot à tabac (literally, a tobacco pot)
a really ugly, stubby woman, a <u>dog</u>	un boudin* (literally, black pudding, a stubby sausage)
mannish (said of a woman)	hommasse
a <u>big fatso</u>	un gros patapouf un gros plein de soupe
a <u>fat slob</u>	un gros lard
to have big tits	avoir du monde au balcon
to <u>be well rounded</u>	être bien roulée être bien balancée être bien carrossée (la carrosserie = the car body)
a handsome morsel	un beau morceau
to be flat-chested	être plate comme une limande (la limande = the sole) être plate comme une planche à pain (literally, to be as flat as a bread board)
to be bald	ne pas avoir un poil sur le caillou
to be going bald	perdre ses plumes se déplumer
a wig	une moumoute
to be hard of hearing	être dur,e de la feuille

35

deaf	sourdingue
to <u>have cauliflower ears</u>	avoir les oreilles en feuille de chou
to be cross-eyed	avoir un oeil qui dit merde à l'autre**
myopic	bigleux, bigleuse
dirty	cracra, crado, cradingue, cradoc (all derived from "crasse" = filth)
to have dirty fingernails	avoir les ongles en deuil (literally, to have one's nails in mourning)

IT'S TIME TO PRACTISE YOUR EXPERTISE

1 Les zizis de vieille bonne femme, ça pue le fauve.

2 Les français ont des pifs énormes.

3 Un beau gosse ne sortirait jamais avec un boudin comme elle.

4 Hé, merde, ça schlingue ici. Y'a un salaud qui a pété! C'est dégueulasse, je vais dégobiller.

5 Ce mec a une gueule qui ne me revient pas.

6 Une gonzesse bien foutue a de longues guiboles, de beaux nichons, un petit cul mignon et un chat parfumé.

7 T'as vu cette espèce d'avorton culotté qui se branle chaque fois qu'il voit la belle Marie?

8 Son paternel a la crève, on dirait qu'il va claquer.

9 Je suis crevé, je vais juste pousser un roupillon.

10 Tes tifs sont drôlement cracra.

1 Old ladies' cunts stink.

2 The French have huge conks.

3 A handsome young thing would never go out with a dog like her.

36

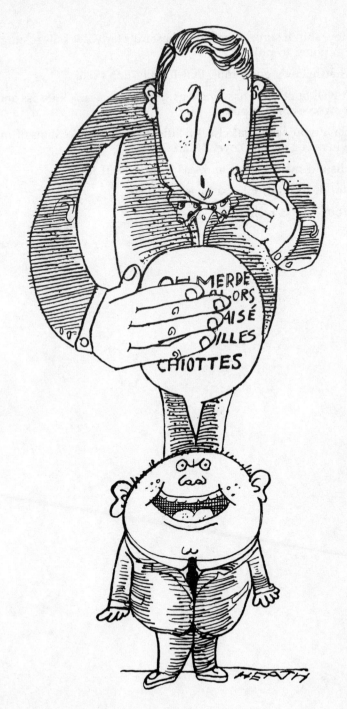

4 Hey, shit, it stinks here! Some bastard's farted! It's disgusting, I'm going to puke.

5 That fellow's got a mug that I really don't like.

6 A well-built chick has long legs, pretty tits, a cute little ass and a sweet-smelling pussy.

7 Have you seen that cheeky little runt who jerks himself off whenever he sees lovely Marie?

8 His old man is ill, it looks as if he'll snuff it.

9 I'm dead-tired, I'll just have a snooze.

10 Your hair is really dirty.

IV THE WEIGHTY MATTERS OF LOVE AND SEX (National Obsession Number One)

The Protagonists

WOMEN

a girl, a bird, a chick	une nana une nénette une gonzesse** une souris*
his girlfriend	sa pépée* sa petite amie
his loved one (ironical)	sa dulcinée
his woman, his <u>broad</u>	sa julie* sa poule**
his old lady (wife)	sa bergère* sa bobonne
an innocent, naive young thing	une oie blanche
a virgin	une pucelle
a spinster	une vieille fille
a coy hypocrite	une sainte nitouche
a shrew	une mégère
a <u>bitch</u>	une garce* une salope**
a stuck-up female	une pimbêche

a cock-teaser	une allumeuse* (from "allumer" = to inflame, to set on fire)
a seductress	une vamp
sexy	sexy
an easy lay	un paillasson* (literally, a doormat)
to be an easy lay	avoir les cuisses légères* (literally, to have light thighs)
a man-eater	une mangeuse d'hommes
a kept woman	une femme soutenue
a scrubber, a slut	une pouffiasse** une roulure**
a whore	une pute* une putain* une morue**
a lady of the night	une fille de joie
a prostitute who solicits from cars	une amazone*
to solicit	racoler
to walk the streets	faire le trottoir faire le tapin* faire de la retape*
a whorehouse	un bordel une maison close une maison de passe un claque*
the madam	la maquerelle*
a dike	une gouine**

MEN

a fellow, a bloke, a chap	un type un gars un mec*
her boyfriend	son petit ami son jules*
a suitor	un soupirant
a virgin	un puceau
a confirmed bachelor	un vieux garçon
a stay-at-home	un pantouflard (from "la pan-toufle" = the slipper)
a male chauvinist pig	un phallocrate (from "le phal-lus") un phallo
a smooth talker	un baratineur
a womaniser	un coureur un cavaleur
one who likes to go on the prowl for a pick-up (but not involving prostitution)	un dragueur
a casanova	un tombeur*
to be a sex maniac	avoir le sang chaud (literally, to be hot-blooded)
a sex maniac	un chaud-lapin* (literally, a hot rabbit) un tringlomane** (from "trin-gler**" = to have it off)
an exhibitionist, a lecher	un satyre
to suffer from middle-aged randiness	avoir le démon de midi*

to be a groper	avoir la main baladeuse (literally, to have a wandering hand)
a cuckold	un cocu*
a gigolo	un gigolo
a <u>pimp</u>	un maquereau* un hareng* (notice the fishy terminology around prostitution, "le maquereau" being literally a mackerel, "le hareng" a herring and in the female section, "la maquerelle" a female mackerel, "la morue" a cod) un souteneur
a <u>fag</u>, a <u>queer</u>	un pédé*, une pédale* (from "le pédéraste") une tante*, une tantouse* (literally, an auntie) une tapette* une lope* une grande folle*, une folle*
a transvestite	un travelot*, un trav*

GENERAL DESCRIPTIVE TERMINOLOGY

sexy	sexy
sex-appeal	le sex-appeal
to be trendy	être dans le vent (literally, to be in the wind, that is, to fly with the wind)
a young trendy	un minet, une minette
to be striking and elegant	avoir du chien avoir de la gueule
to be popular with the opposite sex	avoir du succès auprès du sexe opposé

42

easy-going	relaxe
a stay-at-home	un pot-au-feu ("le pot-au-feu" is a boiled beef and vegetable dish)
a show-off	un m'as-tu-vu
full of oneself	puant,e (remember "puer" = to stink)
snobby, toffy-nosed	snob bêcheur, bêcheuse
fickle	volage
a reveller, a fast liver	un noceur, une noceuse
base, vile	immonde
corrupt	pourri,e (pourri = rotten)
twisted	tordu,e
dirty-minded	cochon, cochonne grossier, grossière
depraved	vicelard,e
obsessed	obsédé,e
repressed	refoulé,e frustré,e
masochistic	maso
to be obsessed with sex	être porté,e sur la chose
to be a cradle-snatcher	les prendre au berceau
to be AC-DC	marcher à la voile et à la vapeur (literally, to function by sail and steam)

43

The Chase

to go on the prowl, to pick up	draguer
to look for some crumpet	chercher un peu de fesse*
to give someone the eye	faire de l'oeil à quelqu'un
to make sheep eyes at someone	faire les yeux doux à quelqu'un
to devour someone with one's eyes	manger quelqu'un des yeux
to ogle	lorgner zieuter (from "les yeux" pronounced "les zieu")
to cast lustful looks on	reluquer*
to hang around, to come sniffing around	rôder autour
to chat up, to sweet-talk	baratiner faire du baratin à faire du plat à faire du gringue à
smooth talk, sweet talk	le baratin
to be taken in by someone's smooth talking	se laisser prendre au baratin de quelqu'un
to catch someone's fancy	taper dans l'oeil de quelqu'un
to make a hit	faire une touche
to flirt	flirter
flirting	le flirt
love at first sight	le coup-de-foudre (literally, the bolt of lightning)

the rendezvous	le rencard
to play footsy with	faire du pied à faire du genou à
to flatter and fondle	faire des mamours à
to feel up	faire des papouilles à
to pet	peloter*
petting	le pelotage*
to paw	tripoter*
to leap on	sauter sur
to neck	se bécoter
a kiss	une bise un bisou un bécot
come and see my etchings	venez voir mes estampes japonaises
my darling	mon chéri, ma chérie mon chou mon petit chou mon cocot, ma cocotte
my darling (woman only)	ma biche (literally, my doe)

Emotions and Conquest

to hit it off	avoir les atomes crochus (literally, to have hooked atoms)
to have a crush on	avoir le béguin pour
to have a soft spot for	avoir un faible pour
to be besotted by	s'enamouracher de

to be smitten by someone	être mordu,e de quelqu'un avoir quelqu'un dans la peau (literally to have someone under one's skin)
to be mad about	être fou, folle de aimer à la folie
to live on love alone	vivre d'amour et d'eau fraîche
to find the man/woman in a million	trouver la perle (literally, to find the pearl) trouver l'oiseau rare (literally, to find the rare bird)
to get one's clutches into	mettre le grapin sur*
to strip	se foutre à poil**
to have it off with, to make love with	s'envoyer* se farcir* se payer* se taper*
to screw, to lay a woman	culbuter une femme* tomber une femme* sauter une femme*
to fuck	baiser** (beware! "le baiser" = the kiss, "embrasser" = to kiss. So never say "je l'ai baisée" when you only mean "I kissed her" because what you are then saying is "I fucked her", a completely different kettle of fish.) tringler**
the bedroom	le baisodrome** (derived from the above)
to get laid	se faire sauter*
to dip one's wick	tremper son biscuit*
a one-night stand	un amour de rencontre

46

a French letter	une capote anglaise (Just let that sink in. It gives you food for thought about the historical antagonism, remembering also that "to take French leave" is "filer à l'anglaise".)
feats	les exploits (m.)
to make love in a slow, conventional, unexciting way	faire l'amour à la papa
to deflower	dépuceler passer à la casserole** (also means "to rape")
to come	jouir** prendre son pied**
climax	l'extase (f.)
to give a blow-job	faire le pompier** faire une pipe**
69	le soixante-neuf**
to bugger	enculer** emmancher** enfoirer**
to make love doggy-style	baiser en levrette** (literally, to fuck like a greyhound bitch)
a sleepless night	une nuit blanche

Parties

to get all dolled/dressed up	se nipper se saper
a party (with dancing)	une surprise-party une surboum une boum

48

to whoop it up	faire la bringue
	faire la bombe
	faira la noce
	faire la foire
	faire la bamboula
	faire la nouba
to carouse	faire ribote
to get an eyeful	se rincer l'oeil
dirty jokes	les histoires paillardes
	les histoires salées
obscenities	les ordures (f.)
	les saletés (f.)
	les horreurs (f.)
a wife-swapping party with two couples	une partie carrée*
an orgy	une partouse*
to participate in an orgy	partouser*
one who likes orgies	un partouzard*
a sexual orgy involving young girls below the age of consent	un ballet rose
a sexual orgy involving young boys below the age of consent	un ballet bleu
to play gooseberry	tenir la chandelle
dirty flicks	les films porno
porno press	la presse du cul**
a dirty newspaper	un journal de fesse*
drugs	la came
a junkie	un camé
a drug addict	un toxico
marijuana	le marie-jeanne

LSD	l'acid
an LSD trip	un trip
a narcotic drug	un stup (short for "le stupéfi-ant" = the narcotic drug)
heroin	la chnouffe*, la schnouff*
to have a fix	se fixer* se schnouffer* se shooter*

Disasters

to be hanging around waiting, to be kicking one's heels	faire le poireau (le poireau = the leek) poireauter
to stand someone up	poser un lapin à quelqu'un
gossip	les ragots (m.)
to gossip	jacter
to lead on	faire marcher
to break hearts	faire des ravages (le ravage = devastation)
to drop, to jilt	plaquer laisser tomber laisser choir
to be down in the dumps, to feel low and depressed	avoir le cafard
melodrama	le mélo
to take someone for a ride	avoir quelqu'un (used most often by the victim in the "passé composé", as in "il m'a eue" = he took me for a ride)

50

to be had	se faire avoir
to come home without having scored	revenir la bitte sous le bras** (remember "la bitte" = the cock?)
to steal someone's girlfriend	souffler la petite amie de quelqu'un
	barboter la petite amie de quelqu'un
	piquer la petite amie de quelqu'un
	pincer la petite amie de quelqu'un
	faucher la petite amie de quelqu'un
to be unfaithful	faire des infidélités
to cuckold	cocufier* (note that "une veine de cocu" = the luck of the devil. It shows that, for the French, being unlucky in love gives you a good chance in other endeavours, so all is not lost and maybe face is saved.)
to put a bun in the oven, to impregnate	encloquer** mettre en cloque** (la cloque = the blister)
to have a bun in the oven, to be pregnant	avoir le ballon*
a backstreet abortionist	une faiseuse d'ange**
to get hitched	se mettre la corde au cou
the mother-in-law	la belle-doche*
a flock of kids	une ribambelle de gosses
the clap	la vérole
	la chtouille**
	la chaude-pisse** (literally, hot-piss)
	la chaude-lance**

NOW GET ON WITH IT

1   Les anglais sont tous des pédés; les français sont des chaud-lapins; les italiens sont des baratineurs.

2   Au fond, les mecs sont tous phallos.

3   Ta copine est une vraie pouffiasse, elle se fait sauter par tout le monde.

4   Fais gaffe au père Dupont: il a le démon de midi, il court après toutes les nanas du bureau, a la main baladeuse et te sautera dessus si tu te trouves seule avec lui.

5   Il est dingue de se mettre la corde au cou: il va se farcir une salope de belle-doche. M'enfin, peut-être qu'il a foutu sa dulcinée en cloque.

6   Y'a que les minables, les refoulés, les pourris et les pauvres cons qui partousent ou se shootent.

7   Quelle bêcheuse, ta frangine, avec tous ses petits minets!

8   Il a le cafard parce que sa nana l'a plaqué après deux ans.

9   Dis, t'as fais une touche avec le type là-bas, il n'arrête pas de te zieuter.

I shouldn't have to give you the translation if you've been studying your vocabulary with diligence. But, anyway, I'll be generous.

1   Englishmen are all fags; Frenchmen are sex maniacs; Italians are smooth talkers.

2   Basically men are all chauvinist pigs.

3   Your friend is a real scrubber, she gets laid by everyone.

4   Watch old man Dupont: he's suffering from the middle-age lust syndrome, he chases all the girls in the office, he's a groper and he'll jump on you if you're alone with him.

5   He's crazy to get hitched: he's going to be landed with a bitch of a mother-in-law. Well, maybe he's got his loved one "in trouble"

6   Only the pathetic, the repressed, the rotten and the poor jerks go to orgies or shoot drugs.

7   What a snob your sister is with her little trendies!

8 He's depressed because his girlfriend dumped him after two years.

9 Hey, you've made a hit with that guy over there, he keeps on ogling you.

V THE NO LESS WEIGHTY MATTERS OF FOOD AND DRINK
(National Obsession Number Two)

food, grub	la bouffe* la boustif* la boustifaille* la graille*
to eat	bouffer* grailler*
to be hungry	avoir la fringale* avoir un creux
to be dying of hunger	crever de faim
it gives one an appetite	ça creuse
shall we start?	alors, on attaque?
a <u>snack</u>	un casse-croûte ("la croûte" here is the end of the long French bread "la baguette"; you would be breaking off a piece of the "baguette" to have a snack with cheese, chocolate, pâté, etc.)
to <u>have a bite</u>	casser la croûte
to have a hearty appetite	avoir un bon coup de fourchette (literally, to have a good way with the fork)
to <u>stuff one's face</u>	s'empiffrer* s'en mettre plein la lampe se taper la cloche

to shovel it in	bouffer à la pelle*
to polish off	se farcir*
	se payer*
a gourmet	une fine-gueule
a glutton	un goinfre
a huge, slap-up meal	un gueuleton*
to be full	caler
to have enough to feed an army	en avoir assez pour un régiment
watery soup	la lavasse* (literally, dishwater)
potatoes	les patates (f.)
beans	les fayots (m.)
cheese	le frometon
	le frome
meat	la bidoche
tough meat	la barbaque*
	la carne*
it's as tough as old boots	c'est de la semelle (la semelle = the sole of a shoe)
to hack away at the roast	charcuter le rôti
salami	le sauciflard
the leftovers	les rogatons
pigswill	la ragougnasse*
a fridge	un frigo
to do the cooking	faire la tambouille*
	faire la popote
awful cooking	la tambouille*

to burn	cramer*
smells of burnt fat	les odeurs (f.) de graillon*
a café	un bistro(t)
a restaurant	un resto
a seedy-looking little eating place	un boui-boui*
a cook	un cuistot*
the bill, the <u>damage</u>	la douleureuse (literally, the painful one)
to <u>fleece the customer</u>	écorcher le client (écorcher = to skin)
this place charges extortionate prices	c'est le coup de fusil ici

Drink

wine	le pinard
red wine	le rouquin (rouquin,e = red-haired)
ordinary red wine	le gros rouge qui tache et qui pousse au crime (literally, the thick red wine that stains and incites to crime) le gros rouge (short for the above)
cheap wine, <u>plonk</u>	la piquette*
a little glass of wine	un petit canon
a litre bottle	un litron
the empties	les cadavres (m.)

weak, low-quality alcohol	la bibine*
rot-gut	le tord-boyaux*
any weak beverage (coffee, etc.)	du pipi* d'âne (literally, donkey's piss) du pipi* de chat (literally, cat's piss)
a drop	une larme (literally, a tear)
galore	à gogo (as in "il y avait du whisky à gogo" = there was whisky galore)
a cocktail	un apéro (short for "un apéritif")
to have a drink	boire un coup prendre un pot
to celebrate an event with a drink	arroser un évènement
this calls for a celebration!	ça s'arrose!
cheers!	tchin tchin!
to be partial to red wine	marcher au rouge carburer au rouge
to dilute one's wine with water	baptiser son vin
to be tipsy	avoir un coup dans l'aile être pompette
to have had one too many	avoir un verre dans le nez
to get pissed	se saouler la gueule** se cuiter* se payer une bonne cuite*
plastered, drunk	paf* rond,e rond,e comme une bille bourré,e*

57

	blindé,e*
	schlass*
to be a <u>boozer</u>	picoler*
a <u>soak</u>	une éponge* (literally, a sponge)
a <u>boozer</u>	un picoleur*
	un soiffard*
	un boit-sans-soif*
a drunkard	un soulard*
	un soulot*
	un poivrot*
to have a hangover	avoir la gueule de bois* (literally, to have a wooden mouth)
to sleep one's drink off	cuver son vin

HOW ABOUT THESE SENTENCES?

1 Qu'est-ce qu'on bouffe? Je crève de faim!

2 Les journalistes, ça picole drôlement.

3 Les anglais sont bien sympas mais leur tambouille est dégueulasse.

4 Venez prendre un pot dimanche.

5 Oh merde, j'ai cramé la bidoche.

6 Les goinfres se sont farcis tout le rôti.

7 On a fait la nouba chez les Dupont: y'avait du champagne à gogo, tout le monde était paf, ça dégueulait partout.

1 What are we eating? I'm dying of hunger!

2 Journalists are real boozers.

3 The English are awfully nice but their cooking is disgusting.

4 Come and have a drink on Sunday.

5 Oh hell, I burnt the meat.

6 The gluttons polished off all the roast.

7 We whooped it up at the Duponts: there was champagne galore, everyone was drunk, people were puking everywhere.

VI AGGRO

With your average Frog bristling with impatience towards all other mortals, it is inevitable that there should be a number of words describing forms of aggression or the threat and result of its use.

<u>chicken</u>	dégonflé,e
to <u>chicken out</u>	se dégonfler (literally, to lose all one's air)
cowardly, lily-livered	froussard,e trouillard,e
fear	la frousse la pétoche la trouille
to be afraid	avoir la frousse avoir la pétoche avoir la trouille avoir les jetons (pronounce this "chton")
to <u>squabble</u>	se chamailler
to get cross	se foutre** en rogne se foutre** en boule
to be hopping mad	être furax* être furibard,e* être furibond,e*
to tell someone off	attraper quelqu'un passer un savon à quelqu'un secouer les puces à quelqu'un (literally, to shake someone's fleas)

	enguirlander*
	engueuler**
to get a telling off	se faire attraper
	se faire passer un savon
	se faire secouer les puces
	se faire enguirlander*
	se faire engueuler**
	se faire sonner les cloches
a row	une prise de bec*
a rumpus	un chahut
to rag the schoolmaster	chahuter le prof

a fight between women — un crêpage de chignon (le chignon = bun, the hairstyle; crêper = to tease, to crimp hair, so you get the image of women tearing at each other's hair in that nasty female way of fighting)

to <u>kick up a stink</u>, to <u>make a racket</u> — faire du boucan / faire du raffut / faire du barouf

to yell — gueuler**

there is going to be trouble — ça va barder / ça va chauffer / il va y avoir du grabuge / il va y avoir de la casse (violent trouble)

things are heating up — ça barde / ça sent le roussi (roussi = burnt, scorched)

to give someone a rough time — faire passer un mauvais quart d'heure à quelqu'un

to be on the verge of doing something nasty — aller faire un malheur (as in "je vais faire un malheur" = I'm

	about to do something horrible)
to be at one another's throats	se bouffer le nez*
to slap	allonger une baffe
	flanquer une baffe
	ficher* une baffe
	foutre** une baffe
a clout	une beigne
	une taloche
	un marron
	une châtaigne
	une pêche
a black eye	un oeil au beurre noir
a knock, a blow	un gnon
to scuffle, to brawl	se bagarrer
a scuffle, a brawl	une bagarre
a spanking	une fessée
to fly at	voler dans les plumes de*
to have a punch-up	se tabasser
	se taper dessus
to punch someone in the face	envoyer le poing à la figure de quelqu'un
to smash someone's face in	casser la figure à quelqu'un*
	casser la gueule à quelqu'un**
	abîmer le portrait de quelqu'un*
	faire une grosse tête à quelqu'un
to give someone a hiding/thrashing	flanquer une trempe/raclée à quelqu'un
	ficher* une trempe/raclée à quelqu'un
	foutre** une trempe/raclée à quelqu'un

to <u>kick up the arse</u>	botter les fesses*
to <u>tear one another's guts out</u>	s'étriper*
to <u>send someone flying</u>	envoyer quelqu'un valser (literally, to send someone waltzing)
to wreck	amocher bousiller
to faint	tomber dans les pommes
to be unconscious	être dans le cirage (le cirage = the boot polish)
to <u>do in</u>, to kill	zigouiller

to eliminate (to get rid of or to kill)	liquider
to <u>bump off</u>	buter descendre
to shoot someone	flinguer quelqu'un foutre** une balle dans la peau* de quelqu'un
a gun	un flingue, un flingot
a police van	un panier à salade
prison	la taule, la tôle

QUIZ TIME

1 Les gosses ont besoin qu'on leur foute des baffes de temps en temps.

2 Espèce de salaud, je vais te casser la gueule.

3 Le mec avait tellement la frousse qu'il est tombé dans les pommes.

4 Les gangsters ont été foutus en taule après avoir descendu leurs rivaux.

5 Je vais me faire secouer les puces parce que j'ai foutu un oeil au beurre noir à mon frangin.

1 Kids need to be slapped from time to time.

2 You bastard, I'll smash your face in.

3 The guy was so scared he fainted.

4 The gangsters were thrown into prison after having bumped off their rivals.

5 I'm going to get a telling off because I gave my brother a black eye.

VII MONEY MATTERS

money	le fric
	le pognon
	le pèze
	la galette
	la braise
	l'oseille (f.)
	les ronds (m.)
	le flouse
loose change	la ferraille (literally, scrap iron)
francs	les balles (f.) (as in "ça coûte quinze balles" = it costs fifteen francs)
10,000 francs	une brique
to be broke	être fauché,e
	être à sec
to not have a bean	ne pas avoir un radis (le radis = radish)
	ne pas avoir un rond
filthy rich	rupin,e*
a spoiled daddy's boy	un fils à papa
to be loaded	être plein,e aux as
mean	radin,e
a skin-flint	un grippe-sous
to fork out	casquer

to blow	claquer
to be had	se faire avoir
to con, to rip off	rouler
	couillonner**
it's a fake, it's imitation	c'est du toc
junk, rubbish	de la camelote
expensive	chéro
free	à l'oeil
profit	le bénef (short for ''le bénéfice'' = the gain, profit)

PRACTICE MAKES PERFECT

1 Dis, t'as du fric à me passer? Je suis fauché et je dois 100 balles à mon copain.

2 Ce petit fils à papa a claqué un pognon fou sur de la camelote.

3 J'ai eu ces billets à l'oeil.

4 Ce salaud t'a roulé: t'as casqué une fortune pour du toc.

1 Hey, have you got any money to lend me? I'm broke and I owe my friend 100 francs.

2 That little daddy's boy blew an awful lot of money on junk.

3 I got these tickets free.

4 That bastard ripped you off: you forked out a fortune on imitation rubbish.

VIII WORK AND SOCIAL STATUS

Work and Jobs

work, the job	le boulot
the workplace	la boîte
to work	bosser boulonner
to work hard	bûcher
hard-working	bûcheur,euse
laziness	la cosse la flemme
lazy	flemmard,e
to be bone-idle	avoir un poil dans la main
a failure	un raté, une ratée
to exploit	faire suer le burnous* (suer = to perspire, le burnous = an Arabian robe-like garment; from the good old days of the Empire when one made the Arabs work like slaves)
to sack , to kick out	vider (literally, empty out) foutre** à la porte
to have friends in the right places	avoir du piston
string-pulling	le piston

to pull strings on behalf of someone	pistonner quelqu'un
to grease someone's palm	graisser la patte à quelqu'un*
a bigwig	une grosse légume un gros bonnet une huile
a cop, a policeman	un flic un poulet
the fuzz, the police	la flicaille*
down with the pigs!	mort aux vaches!**
a cop on two wheels	une vache à roulettes**
a member of the security/ espionage services	un barbouze
a bodyguard	un gorille
a quack	un toubib*
a teacher	un prof
a chef	un cuistot*
a funeral parlour employee	un croque-mort* (croquer = to bite into, to munch)
a priest in his cassock	un corbeau* (literally, a crow)
a politician	un politicard*
a lady lavatory attendant	une dame-pipi*
a cobbler	un bouif*
a painter (the artistic sort)	un barbouilleur* (barbouiller = to smear, to scrawl)
third-rate paintings	les croûtes* (f.)
a third-rate book, film or other work of art	un navet

| a paper-pusher (usually a bureaucrat) | un rond-de-cuir* |
| a soldier | un troufion* |

Social Status and Political Affiliation

a <u>hick</u>, a <u>bumpkin</u>	un plouc, une ploucquesse*
	un pécore*
	un péquenaud*
	un pedzouille*

69

a peasant	un cul-terreux** (literally, one whose arse is covered in earth)
	un bouseux** (from "la bouse de vache" = cow dung)
the country (as opposed to the city)	la cambrousse*
the <u>sticks</u>	la brousse*
a village	un patelin*
a <u>real hole</u>	un trou*
	un bled*
to live in the back of beyond	habiter au feu de dieu
	habiter à perpète ("perpète" is short for "la perpétuité", conveying the notion of great distance)
a tramp	un clodo*
the lower classes, the masses	le populo*
a <u>prole</u> (proletarian)	un prolo*
an aristocrat	un aristo*
the <u>upper crust</u>	le gratin
a Parisian	un parigot, une parigote* (Parisians hold a high rank in the social hierarchy; provincials are considered virtually subhuman)
a reactionary	un réac*
a fascist	un facho*
a <u>commie</u>	un coco*
an anarchist	un anar*

a <u>demo</u>   une manif (short for "la manifestation" = the demonstration)

TEST YOUR KNOWLEDGE

1 Les seules gonzesses qui sont promues dans cette sale boîte sont les pouffiasses qui se laissent baiser par le patron ou les salopes qui ont du piston.

2 Les toubibs donnent beaucoup de boulot aux croque-morts.

3 Un plouc, ça se voit à dix mètres.

4 La punition la plus sévère pour les aristos, à l'époque des rois, c'était l'exil à la cambrousse.

5 Comment, ma fille épouser un cul-terreux et aller habiter à perpète dans un bled perdu? Pas question.

6 A la manif, les fachos ont foutu une trempe aux cocos.

1 The only women who get promoted in this damn company are the sluts who let the boss screw them or the bitches who have friends in the right places.

2 Quacks give a lot of work to undertakers.

3 You can tell a hick ten metres away.

4 In the days of the kings the most severe punishment for the aristocrats was exile to the country.

5 What, my daughter marry a peasant and live in the back of beyond, in some godforsaken hole? Certainly not.

6 At the demo the fascists gave the commies a thrashing.

IX INDULGING IN RACISM, XENOPHOBIA AND DISRESPECT FOR ONE'S ELDERS

Despite the centuries of animosity between the English and the French, Froggies have been unable to come up with any derogatory term for English or British. The pathetic expressions "les rosbifs" (the roast beefs) or "les biftecks" (the steaks) are hardly likely to set the blood boiling; they are not used a great deal anyway. To be sure, it is better to be known as a beef-eater than as a devourer of slithery, vile frogs. That the French consider the English to be double-dealers, hypocrites and experts in the art of the underhand trick comes through in their use of "la perfide Albion" (perfidious Albion) to designate Britain and of "filer à l'anglaise" for "to take French leave" (ha!), but for the individual Englishman there is no venomous word.

a kraut	un boche** un chleuh** un fritz** un frisé** un fridolin**
a dago	un rastaquouère** (this has generally meant a greasy foreigner but usually equals dago)
a wop	un rital** un macaroni**
a yank	un amerloque* un amerluche* un ricain*
a Russian	un ruski* un ruskof*
a chink	un chinetoque**

a <u>wog</u>, a <u>nigger</u>	un bougnoule** un moricaud** un nègre*
an Arab	un bougnoule** un bicot**
a North African Arab (the French bugbear)	un raton** (gives rise to "la ratonnade" = mob Arab-bashing) un melon** un crouille** un noraf
a <u>kike</u>	un youpin** un youtre**
Jewish	baptisé au sécateur* (literally, baptised with pruning shears)
a <u>prod</u>	un parpaillot*
an <u>old grandad</u>	un vieux pépé*
an <u>old granny</u>	une vieille mémé*
an <u>old biddy</u>	une vieille toupie*
an <u>old fogey</u>	un vieux schnoque* un vieux bonze*
an <u>old hag</u>, a <u>crone</u>	une vieille bique* (la bique = the nanny-goat) une vieille rombière* une vieille taupe*
to speak pidgin French	parler petit nègre parler le français comme une vache espagnole

HERE IS ANOTHER EXERCISE FOR YOU

1 Les boches bossent dur, mais les ritals sont flemmards.

2 C'est vrai que les nègres ont de grandes verges?

3 Les amerloques sont de grands enfants.

4 Les medias, c'est rempli de youpins.

5 C'est un quartier de ratons.

6 Allez, bouge ton cul, vieille bique.

7 Moi, j'peux pas sentir les vieux schnoques.

1 Krauts work hard, but wops are lazy.

2 Is it true that niggers have big cocks?

3 Americans are big kids.

4 The media are full of kikes.

5 It's an Arab neighbourhood.

6 Come on, move your arse, old hag.

7 I can't stand old fogeys.

X TO EXIT RAPIDLY

to push off, to get the hell out   filer
se barrer
se tailler
se tirer
déguerpir
se débiner
ficher*/foutre** le camp

to hurry up   se magner
se dégrouiller
se grouiller

on your way! get out!   allez, oust!
dégagez!
débarrassez le plancher!

to kick out   vider
balancer
foutre** à la porte

APPLY YOUR KNOWLEDGE

1 Hé, les mômes, foutez-moi le camp d'ici! Allez, magnez-vous ou j'appelle les flics.

2 Filons avant que la maternelle n'arrive.

1 Hey, kids, clear off! Come on, hurry up or I'll call the cops.

2 Let's get the hell out of here before the old lady comes.

XI POSITIVE THINKING

Although the Frenchman's bent is for the scathing remark, he *is* able to whip up enthusiasm.

great, fantastic (used as an adjective or as an exclamation)	formidable, formide
	terrible
	sensas (short for "sensation-nel"
	super
	génial,e
	chouette (when used as an adjective, it is placed before the noun, not after as others are)
	impeccable
	au poil (don't confuse with "à poil" which, as you no doubt remember, means "naked")
	extra
great, fantastic (used only as an adjective)	bath
	chié,e**
	chiadé,e**
	du tonnerre
to have great success	avoir un succès boeuf
to have great effect	avoir un effet boeuf

TRY YOUR HAND AT THESE SENTENCES

1 Chouette, les vacances sont arrivées!

2 Elle est super, ta bagnole!

3 J'ai lu un bouquin sensas.

4 Elle est chouette, ta frangine!

5 Cette pièce a eu un succès boeuf.

1 Great, the holidays are here!

2 Your car is fantastic!

3 I read a fabulous book.

4 Your sister is great!

5 This play had tremendous success.

XII FOREIGN INVASIONS OF THE LANGUAGE

READ THE FOLLOWING

1 C'est un appartement de grand standing, avec parking.

2 Quel était le score au match?

3 Les gangsters ont effectué un raid pendant le meeting. Le hold-up leur a rapporté 10000 dollars.

4 J'ai acheté ce gadget au stand du fond.

5 Au club, certains étaient en smoking, d'autres en jeans et pull.

6 J'ai acheté un sandwich au self-service.

7 Le cameraman a pris des films pendant l'interview.

8 Le leader du parti souffre de stress.

9 On a fait du stop.

Recognise some of the words? "Franglais", that insidious creeping of English words into the French language, is a source of worry to the French authorities but is proving hard to contain. All the words above are used in conversation and in the media; they aren't considered colloquial. Therefore the above sentences are not an attempt at being funny, they are examples of contemporary French! In passing from English to French, however, some words have undergone a little transformation, so here are the translations:

1 It's a luxury flat with parking facilities.

2 What was the score at the match?

3 The gangsters carried out a raid during the meeting. The hold-up netted them 10,000 dollars.

4 I bought this gadget at the stand at the back.

5 At the club some were wearing dinner jackets, others jeans and sweaters.

6 I bought a sandwich at the self-service restaurant.

7 The cameraman filmed during the interview.

8 The party's leader is suffering from stress.

9 We hitchhiked.

From the former North African colonies come some Arab words which are firmly implanted in French colloquial vocabulary:

no; no way; nothing	oualou
a hole (the village-in-the-sticks type, remember?)	un bled*
the same	kif-kif
a little (quantity)	un chouïa
luck	la baraka
not much, nothing much	pas bézef
the boss	le caïd
money	le flouse

IMPROVE YOUR COLLOQUIAL USAGE FROM THE FOLLOWING

1 "Vous prenez du café?" "Un chouïa."

2 Y'a pas bézef à faire dans ce bled.

3 "Tu veux le rouge ou le bleu?" "Oh, n'importe, c'est kif-kif."

4 Le caïd a de la baraka.

1 "Will you have some coffee?" "A little."

79

2 There's not much to do in this hole.

3 "Do you want the red one or the blue one?" "Oh, it doesn't matter, it's the same."

4 The boss has luck on his side.

XIII YOUR FINAL EXAM

Identify the literary tales or historical figures. Answers, but not translations, are provided on the following page.

1   Ce mec devait être vachement frustré parce que c'était un nabot. Sa bergère, qui était un peu bougnoule sur les bords, voulait toujours qu'il la baise, mais il répondait "Pas ce soir, Josephine" parce qu'il était toujours en train de se bagarrer (avec les boches, les ruskis, etc.). Elle l'a cocufié. Les anglais lui ont foutu une vraie trempe, l'ont exilé dans un bled infâme et l'ont probablement empoisonné avec leur tambouille infecte.

2   Y'a deux familles d'aristos ritals qui sont en rogne et puis le fiston de l'une a le béguin pour la fille de l'autre. Il se la farcit, mais ils ont la frousse de dire à leurs vieux qu'ils sont enamourachés, alors ils se zigouillent. A la fin, toute la bande de cons chiale et devient copains.

3   Un piaf avait chipé un frome et allait juste le bouffer quand un renard fait un peu de lèche-cul pour lui faire ouvrir la gueule. Le frome tombe, le renard le pique et déguerpit avec.

4   C'était un roi, un gros lard mais pas con. Il est devenu parpaillot pour balancer sa bobonne, dont il avait ras le bol. D'autres bobonnes, quand elles l'emmerdaient, il les a faites zigouiller.

ASSESSMENT

0 correct = Connard!
1 correct = Dégueulasse!
2 correct = Flemmard!
3 correct = Sympa!
4 correct = Sensas!